Mastering the Art of Self-Growth

TABLE OF CONTENTS

➤ **Chapter 5:**

The Power of Habit
- Understanding Habit Formation
- Crafting Habits that Propel Growth

➤ **Chapter 6:**

Lifelong Learning
- The Importance of Continuous Education
- Tools and Techniques for Effective Learning

➤ **Chapter 7:**

Nurturing Relationships
- The Role of Relationships in Personal Growth
- Building and Maintaining Meaningful Connections

➤ **Chapter 8:**

The Role of Mentorship

WHY SELF-GROWTH MATTERS

In an ever-evolving world, the importance of self-growth cannot be overstated. It is the driving force behind personal development, leading to a more fulfilling, meaningful, and successful life. But why does self-growth matter so much?

........here are some compelling reasons:

Why Self-Growth Matters

Personal Fulfillment: At its core, self-growth is about becoming the best version of oneself. It's about recognizing one's potential and working towards realizing it. This journey brings a sense of accomplishment and satisfaction that is unparalleled.

Adaptability: The world is constantly changing, and those who commit to self-growth are better equipped to adapt to these changes. Whether it's technological advancements, shifts in job markets, or personal life changes, growth-oriented individuals can navigate these transitions with greater ease.

Improved Relationships: As we grow and evolve, we become better communicators, listeners, and partners. Self-growth often leads to improved emotional intelligence, which is crucial for building and maintaining healthy relationships.

Career Advancement: In the professional realm, those who are dedicated to personal development often find more opportunities coming their way. They are more likely to be recognized for promotions, be given challenging assignments, and be seen as leaders.

Resilience: Life is full of challenges. Those who prioritize self-growth develop a resilience that helps them face setbacks with courage and optimism. They see challenges as opportunities for further growth rather than insurmountable obstacles.

Lifelong Learning: The pursuit of self-growth fosters a love for learning. Individuals who value growth are always curious, always looking to learn something new, and always seeking to improve. This mindset not only enriches their personal lives but also makes them invaluable in professional settings.

Enhanced Well-being: Numerous studies have shown that personal development is closely linked to mental and physical well-being. Setting and achieving personal goals, embracing new challenges, and continuous learning can lead to increased happiness and reduced stress levels.

Legacy Building: People who prioritize self-growth often leave a lasting impact on their communities and the world at large. They inspire others with their journey, share their knowledge, and contribute positively to society.

Greater Self-awareness: The journey of self-growth is also a journey of self-discovery. It allows individuals to understand their strengths, weaknesses, passions, and fears. This self-awareness is the foundation for making meaningful changes in one's life.

Empowerment: Lastly, self-growth is empowering. It gives individuals the tools, knowledge, and confidence to take control of their destiny, make informed decisions, and live life on their terms.

In conclusion, self-growth is not just a personal journey; it's a journey that has ripple effects. It benefits the individual, their close circles, and the broader community. In a world that can sometimes seem chaotic and unpredictable, self-growth stands as a beacon, guiding individuals to lead richer, more purposeful lives.

CHAPTER 1:

Understanding Your Starting Point

THE POWER OF SELF-AWARENESS

In the vast landscape of personal development, self-awareness stands as a towering beacon. It's the foundation upon which all other growth-oriented qualities are built. But what exactly is self-awareness, and why is it so powerful? Let's delve into the transformative power of understanding oneself.

What is Self-Awareness?

Self-awareness is the conscious knowledge of one's own character, feelings, desires, and motivations. It's the ability to objectively analyze your behaviors, patterns, and habits. It's about understanding your strengths and weaknesses, your triggers and reactions, and the underlying reasons for your actions.

Why is Self-Awareness Important?

Foundation for Growth: Before you can change or improve, you need to know where you stand. Self-awareness provides a clear picture of your current self, allowing you to chart a path for growth effectively.

Improved Decision Making: When you understand your motivations and desires, you can make decisions that align with your true self. This leads to choices that are more fulfilling and beneficial in the long run.

Enhanced Relationships: By understanding yourself, you can communicate better, set clear boundaries, and empathize with others. This leads to healthier, more meaningful relationships.

Emotional Regulation: Recognizing your emotional triggers and understanding why you feel a certain way helps in managing and controlling those emotions. This is crucial for mental well-being and effective interpersonal interactions.

Authenticity: Self-aware individuals are genuine. They act in ways consistent with their beliefs and values, earning the trust and respect of others.

How to Cultivate Self-Awareness?

Reflection: Regular introspection, whether through journaling, meditation, or simply quiet contemplation, can reveal patterns and behaviors.

Feedback: Sometimes, an external perspective can provide insights that we might miss. Seeking feedback from trusted friends, family, or colleagues can be invaluable.

Mindfulness Practices: Engaging in mindfulness exercises, like meditation, helps in staying present and recognizing our thoughts and feelings as they arise.

Professional Guidance: Therapists and counselors can offer tools and frameworks to better understand oneself.

Continuous Learning: Reading books, attending workshops, or taking courses on personal development can provide insights into human behavior and motivations.

THE TRANSFORMATIVE POWER OF SELF-AWARENESS

Self-awareness is not just about understanding oneself; it's about transformation. When you're self-aware:

You're in control, not your impulses.

You understand why you're feeling a certain way and can choose how to react.

You align your actions with your values, leading to a life of purpose and meaning.

In essence, self-awareness is the compass that guides you through the complexities of life. It helps you navigate challenges, build strong relationships, and lead a life that resonates with who you truly are. In a world filled with distractions and external pressures, the power of self-awareness is the key to living authentically and meaningfully.

The small steps matter....

TOOLS FOR SELF-REFLECTION

In today's fast-paced world, taking a moment to pause and reflect can seem like a luxury. However, self-reflection is an essential practice for personal growth, self-awareness, and overall well-being. It allows individuals to understand their actions, feelings, and thoughts more deeply, leading to more informed decisions and a clearer sense of purpose. Here, we explore various tools that can aid in the self-reflection process.

Journaling

One of the most traditional and effective tools for self-reflection, journaling provides a private space to express thoughts, feelings, and experiences. Whether you're jotting down daily events, exploring your emotions, or simply brainstorming, the act of writing can offer clarity and perspective.

Benefits:

Helps in organizing thoughts.

Provides a record of personal growth over time.

Encourages honesty and deep introspection.

Meditation

Meditation, especially mindfulness meditation, is a practice that centers on the present moment. It encourages individuals to observe their thoughts and feelings without judgment.

Benefits:

Enhances self-awareness.

Reduces stress and anxiety.

Improves focus and concentration.

Guided Reflection

There are numerous apps and online platforms that offer guided reflection sessions. These sessions, often led by experts, provide prompts and structure to the reflection process.

Benefits:

Provides direction for those new to self-reflection.

Can introduce different perspectives and techniques.

Offers a structured approach to deep introspection.

Artistic Expression

Drawing, painting, music, dance, or any other form of artistic expression can be a powerful tool for self-reflection. It allows individuals to communicate emotions and thoughts that might be challenging to express in words.

Benefits:

Encourages creativity.

Provides a non-verbal outlet for emotions.

Can lead to unexpected insights.

Nature Walks

The simple act of walking in nature, away from the distractions of daily life, can be therapeutic. Nature offers a serene environment conducive to reflection.

Benefits:

Connects individuals with the natural world.

Reduces stress and clears the mind.

Encourages a broader perspective on personal issues.

Therapy and Counseling

Professional therapists and counselors are trained to guide individuals through the self-reflection process. They can offer tools, techniques, and perspectives that can deepen the understanding of oneself.

Benefits:

Provides expert guidance.

Offers a safe space to discuss personal issues.

Introduces structured techniques for introspection.

Peer Reflection Groups

Joining a group where members share their experiences and reflections can provide diverse perspectives. Such groups offer support, understanding, and often, valuable insights from peers.

Benefits:

Encourages sharing and open communication.

Provides diverse perspectives on common issues.

Builds a sense of community and support.

Conclusion

Self-reflection is a journey inward, a quest to understand oneself better. While the path of introspection is deeply personal, the tools mentioned above can serve as guiding lights, helping individuals navigate the complexities of their inner world. Whether you're a seasoned self-reflector or just beginning your journey, these tools can enhance the depth and clarity of your introspective endeavors.

Setting the vision

DREAMING BEYOND BOUNDARIES

In a world defined by limitations, boundaries, and constraints, the act of dreaming beyond what's immediately possible stands as a testament to the indomitable human spirit. It's the dreamers who have pushed humanity forward, challenging the status quo and envisioning a world beyond the immediate horizon. This article delves into the importance of dreaming beyond boundaries and the transformative power such dreams can have on individuals and societies.

The Essence of Boundless Dreams

Dreaming beyond boundaries means allowing one's imagination to transcend the limitations set by society, circumstances, or even self-doubt. It's about envisioning possibilities that might seem impossible at the moment but have the potential to reshape the future.

Why Dream Beyond Boundaries?

Innovation and Progress: Every significant advancement in history, from the invention of the wheel to space exploration, began as a dream. It was the dreamers who imagined possibilities beyond the known and dared to make them a reality.

Personal Growth: Dreaming big challenges individuals to push their limits, learn new skills, and step out of their comfort zones. It fosters resilience, determination, and a growth mindset.

Inspiration to Others: When one person dares to dream big and chase those dreams, it serves as an inspiration to others. It sends a message that boundaries are meant to be challenged and that the impossible can become possible.

Overcoming Adversity: Boundless dreams provide hope and motivation, especially during challenging times. They act as a beacon, guiding individuals through obstacles and adversities.

Challenges of Dreaming Big

While dreaming beyond boundaries has its merits, it's not without challenges:

Skepticism from Others: Society often resists change, and dreamers might face skepticism or even ridicule from those who adhere to the status quo.

Fear of Failure: The bigger the dream, the greater the risk. The fear of failure can be a significant deterrent for many.

Resource Constraints: Grand dreams often require significant resources, be it time, money, or effort.

Cultivating Boundless Dreams

Nurture Curiosity: Stay curious about the world, always seeking to learn and explore. Curiosity is the seed from which big dreams grow.

Surround Yourself with Dreamers: Being around like-minded individuals who believe in dreaming big can be incredibly motivating. They provide support, share insights, and challenge you to think bigger.

Set Clear Goals: While dreaming is essential, it's equally crucial to set clear, actionable goals to turn those dreams into reality.

Embrace Failure: Instead of fearing failure, see it as a learning opportunity. Every setback offers a lesson that brings you one step closer to your dream.

Stay Resilient: The path to realizing big dreams is often fraught with challenges. Resilience and perseverance are key.

Conclusion

Dreaming beyond boundaries is more than just wishful thinking; it's a call to action. It's a challenge to individuals and societies to think bigger, aim higher, and push the limits of what's possible. In the words of T.E. Lawrence, "All men dream, but not equally. Those who dream by night in the dusty recesses of their minds, wake in the day to find that it was vanity: but the dreamers of the day are dangerous men, for they may act on their dreams with open eyes, to make them possible." So, dare to dream beyond boundaries, for in those dreams lies the future's potential.

CRAFTING YOUR PERSONAL VISION STATEMENT

In the vast expanse of life's journey, a personal vision statement serves as a guiding star, illuminating the path toward one's true aspirations and ideals. Much like a lighthouse guiding ships safely to shore, a well-crafted vision statement can steer you towards your desired destination, even amidst life's storms. This article delves into the art and science of crafting a compelling personal vision statement.

What is a Personal Vision Statement?

A personal vision statement is a clear and concise declaration of an individual's foremost aspirations, values, and goals. It encapsulates not just what you want to achieve, but who you want to become in terms of character, impact, and personal fulfillment.

....why is it Important?

Clarity: It provides clarity about what you truly want from life, helping you to focus your energy and resources effectively.

Motivation: During challenging times, revisiting your vision statement can reignite your passion and drive.

Decision-making: It acts as a benchmark, helping you make decisions that align with your long-term aspirations.

Personal Growth: It challenges you to think deeply about your values and aspirations, fostering introspection and personal growth.

STEPS TO CRAFT YOUR PERSONAL VISION STATEMENT

Self-reflection: Begin with introspection. Ask yourself:

What are my core values?

What kind of person do I want to become?

What impact do I want to have on my community or the world?

What personal, professional, and spiritual goals do I aspire to achieve?

Visualize: Close your eyes and imagine your ideal future. *Where are you? What are you doing? Who is with you? How do you feel?*

Write Freely: Initially, don't worry about crafting the perfect statement. Write freely, capturing all your thoughts. This raw material will be refined later.

Be Specific: General statements like "*I want to be successful*" are too vague. Instead, focus on specifics, such as "*I want to become a pediatrician serving underprivileged communities.*"

Keep it Concise: A vision statement should be brief, ideally one to two sentences. It should be something you can easily recall and reflect upon.

Seek Feedback: Share your draft with trusted friends or mentors. They might offer insights or perspectives you hadn't considered.

Revise and Refine: Based on your reflections and feedback, refine your statement until it resonates deeply with you.

Revisit Regularly: As you grow and evolve, your vision might change. Regularly revisit and revise your statement to ensure it remains aligned with your aspirations.

EXAMPLES OF PERSONAL VISION STATEMENTS

"To live a life driven by compassion and integrity, leading by example and fostering a world where individuals can thrive irrespective of their backgrounds."

"To harness the power of technology in bridging educational gaps, ensuring every child has access to quality education."

Conclusion

Crafting a personal vision statement is a profound exercise in self-awareness and goal-setting. It's not just about defining a destination but understanding the essence of the journey you wish to undertake. As you navigate the complexities of life, let your vision statement be the compass that keeps you aligned with your true north. Remember, it's not just about reaching a destination, but who you become along the way.

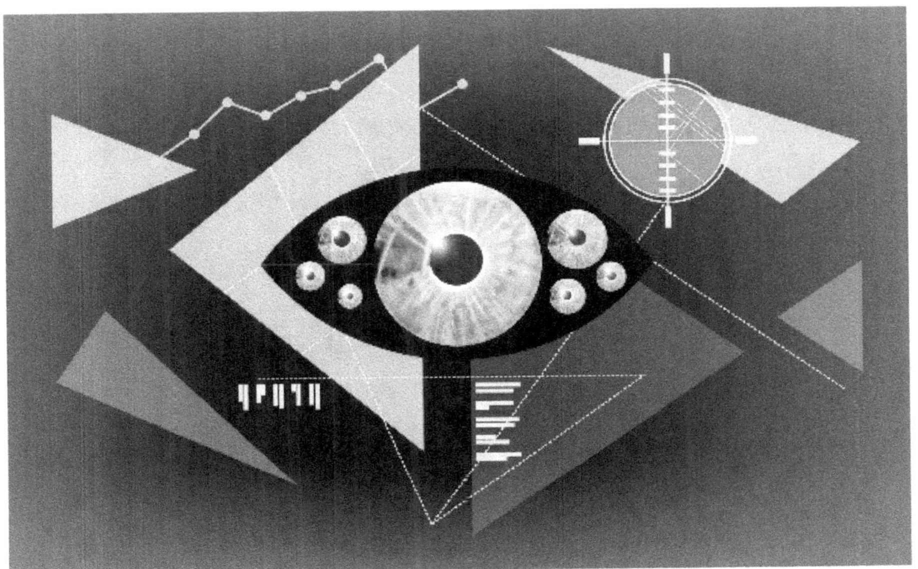

CHAPTER 3:

Overcoming Internal Barriers

THE MINDSET OF LIMITATION

Throughout history, human progress has been marked by our ability to overcome limitations, whether they be physical, technological, or societal. However, one of the most insidious and often overlooked barriers to progress is the mindset of limitation—a self-imposed mental barrier that restricts potential and stifles growth. This article delves into the nature of this mindset, its origins, and strategies to overcome it.

WHAT IS THE MINDSET OF LIMITATION?

The mindset of limitation is a belief system that convinces individuals they cannot achieve certain goals or that they are confined to a particular set of circumstances. This mindset manifests in thoughts like *"I can't," "It's impossible,"* or *"That's just the way things are."*

Origins of the Limiting Mindset

Past Failures: Previous unsuccessful attempts at tasks can lead individuals to believe they lack the capability to succeed in the future.

Societal and Cultural Norms: Societal expectations and stereotypes can impose perceived boundaries on individuals based on factors like gender, race, or socioeconomic status.

Fear of the Unknown: Stepping into unfamiliar territory can be daunting, leading many to avoid challenges altogether.

Overprotective Upbringing: Growing up in an environment where risks are discouraged can lead to a fear of failure and a reluctance to venture outside one's comfort zone.

CONSEQUENCES OF THE LIMITING MINDSET

Stunted Personal Growth: By avoiding challenges, individuals miss out on opportunities for learning and personal development.

Missed Opportunities: A limiting mindset can prevent individuals from seizing potential opportunities for fear of failure or rejection.

Decreased Well-being: Constant self-doubt and feelings of inadequacy can lead to decreased mental well-being and overall life satisfaction.

OVERCOMING THE MINDSET OF LIMITATION

Self-awareness: Recognizing and acknowledging limiting beliefs is the first step towards overcoming them.

Challenge Negative Thoughts: Whenever a limiting thought arises, challenge its validity. Ask yourself, "Is this belief based on facts or assumptions?"

Set Small Goals: Break down larger tasks into smaller, manageable goals. Celebrate each achievement, no matter how minor.

Seek Inspiration: Surround yourself with stories and individuals who have overcome limitations. Let their journeys inspire and motivate you.

Affirmations: Use positive affirmations to rewire your brain. Repeatedly telling yourself "I can" and "I am capable" can gradually replace limiting beliefs.

Seek Support: Talk to mentors, friends, or professionals who can offer guidance, encouragement, and a fresh perspective.

Conclusion

The mindset of limitation, while deeply ingrained in many, is not an insurmountable barrier. With awareness, determination, and the right strategies, it's possible to break free from these self-imposed chains. Remember, the only true limitations are the ones we place on ourselves. By shifting our mindset, we can unlock a world of potential and possibilities. As the saying goes, "Whether you think you can, or you think you can't—you're right." Choose to believe in your boundless potential.

STRATEGIES TO OVERCOME SELF-DOUBT

Self-doubt, that nagging voice of uncertainty, has held many of us back from reaching our full potential. It questions our abilities, undermines our efforts, and paints a bleak picture of our future endeavors. However, while self-doubt is a common human experience, it doesn't have to dictate our actions or outcomes. This article explores actionable strategies to confront and overcome self-doubt, empowering you to move forward with confidence.

UNDERSTANDING SELF-DOUBT

At its core, self-doubt is a fear-based response. It might stem from past failures, negative feedback, or societal pressures. While occasional self-doubt can be a useful tool for self-reflection and improvement, chronic self-doubt can be debilitating, preventing us from taking risks or pursuing our passions.

STRATEGIES TO OVERCOME SELF-DOUBT

Acknowledge and Label Your Feelings: Recognizing and naming your feelings is the first step in addressing them. When you feel self-doubt creeping in, acknowledge it. Say to yourself, "This is self-doubt," and understand it's just a feeling, not a fact.

Challenge Negative Thoughts: Instead of accepting negative thoughts at face value, challenge them. Ask yourself:
Is this thought based on facts or assumptions?
What evidence do I have that supports or contradicts this belief?
Have I succeeded in similar situations before?

Visualize Success: Instead of imagining worst-case scenarios, visualize a successful outcome. Picture yourself achieving your goals and bask in the positive emotions associated with that success.

Affirmations: Positive affirmations can rewire your brain to challenge and combat self-doubt. Repeating phrases like "I am capable," "I believe in myself," or "I am worthy of success" can gradually shift your mindset.

Seek Feedback: Talk to trusted friends, mentors, or colleagues about your feelings of self-doubt. They can provide an external perspective, highlight your strengths, and offer constructive feedback.

Avoid Comparison: In the age of social media, it's easy to compare ourselves to others. Remember that everyone is on their own unique journey, and comparing your behind-the-scenes to someone else's highlight reel is a recipe for self-doubt.

Celebrate Small Wins: Recognize and celebrate your achievements, no matter how minor they may seem. These small victories build confidence and momentum.

Educate and Prepare: Often, self-doubt arises from a fear of the unknown. By educating yourself and preparing adequately for tasks, you can reduce uncertainty and bolster confidence.

Practice Self-compassion: Treat yourself with the same kindness and understanding as you would a dear friend. Remember that everyone, even the most successful individuals, experiences self-doubt from time to time.

Seek Professional Help: If self-doubt is severely impacting your well-being or daily functioning, consider seeking therapy or counseling. Professionals can provide tools and strategies tailored to your specific needs.

CONCLUSION

Overcoming self-doubt is a journey, not a destination. While it might never disappear entirely, with the right strategies, you can diminish its power over you. By confronting and challenging self-doubt, you pave the way for growth, success, and a more confident self. Remember, believing in yourself is the first step to achieving any goal. Embrace your potential, and don't let self-doubt hold you back.

EMBRACING FAILURE AS A TEACHER

In a world that often glorifies success and shuns failure, it's easy to develop a fear of making mistakes. However, if we shift our perspective and view failure not as a dead end but as a teacher, we unlock a powerful tool for personal and professional growth. This article delves into the transformative power of embracing failure as a valuable educator.

REDEFINING FAILURE

Before we can truly embrace failure, we must first redefine it. Instead of seeing it as a definitive statement of our abilities or worth, we should view it as a temporary setback, a lesson, or a stepping stone on the path to success.

WHY FAILURE IS AN INVALUABLE TEACHER

Provides Real-world Experience: While theoretical knowledge is essential, real-world experience, including failures, offers insights that books and lectures cannot.

Fosters Resilience: Facing and overcoming failures builds resilience. It teaches us to bounce back, adapt, and persevere in the face of adversity.

Encourages Innovation: Many groundbreaking inventions and discoveries were born from failures. When one approach doesn't work, it pushes us to think outside the box and innovate.

Highlights Weaknesses: Failure shines a light on areas that need improvement, allowing us to understand our weaknesses and work on them.

Builds Character: Handling failure with grace, humility, and a determination to try again shapes our character and instills values like grit and tenacity.

STRATEGIES TO EMBRACE FAILURE AS A TEACHER

Shift Your Mindset: Cultivate a growth mindset, where challenges are seen as opportunities to learn and grow rather than threats.

Analyze the Failure: Instead of ruminating on the negative emotions, objectively analyze the failure. Ask yourself:

WHAT WENT WRONG?

What could I have done differently?

What can I learn from this experience?

Seek Feedback: Share your experience with mentors, peers, or colleagues. They might offer a fresh perspective or insights you hadn't considered.

Document the Lessons: Maintain a journal or log of your failures and the lessons they taught you. Over time, you'll have a valuable repository of experiences and insights.

Celebrate the Effort: Instead of just celebrating successes, also celebrate the effort, determination, and courage it took to try, even if it resulted in failure.

Practice Self-compassion: Be kind to yourself. Remember that everyone, from novices to experts, experiences failure. It's a universal part of the human experience.

CONCLUSION

Embracing failure as a teacher is about shifting our perspective from fear of mistakes to a love of learning. It's about understanding that the road to success is paved with setbacks, each one offering invaluable lessons. As the renowned inventor Thomas Edison once said, "I have not failed. I've just found 10,000 ways that won't work." By viewing failure through this lens, we not only reduce the fear associated with it but also harness its power to propel us forward. So, the next time you face a setback, remember: failure is not the opposite of success; it's a part of it.

CHAPTER 4:

BUILDING RESILIENCE

THE ROLE OF ADVERSITY IN GROWTH: TURNING CHALLENGES INTO CATALYSTS

Adversity, often perceived as a negative force, has been an integral part of the human experience throughout history. While it's natural to view challenges and setbacks with apprehension, adversity, when approached with the right mindset, can be a powerful catalyst for growth. This article delves into the transformative role adversity plays in personal and collective development.

UNDERSTANDING ADVERSITY

Adversity encompasses a range of challenging situations, from personal setbacks like job loss or health issues to broader societal challenges like wars, economic downturns, or natural disasters. It tests our resilience, patience, and adaptability.

WHY ADVERSITY IS CRUCIAL FOR GROWTH

Builds Resilience: Facing and overcoming challenges strengthens our ability to cope with future adversities. Each setback provides lessons, equipping us with tools to handle similar situations in the future.

Fosters Empathy: Experiencing hardships can deepen our understanding and compassion for others undergoing similar challenges. It bridges gaps, fostering a sense of shared humanity.

Encourages Innovation: Necessity is the mother of invention. Adversity often pushes individuals and societies to think outside the box, leading to groundbreaking innovations and solutions.

Promotes Self-awareness: Adversity acts as a mirror, reflecting our strengths, weaknesses, values, and aspirations. It forces introspection, helping us understand ourselves better.

Strengthens Character: Facing challenges with courage, integrity, and perseverance shapes our character. It instills virtues like grit, determination, and humility.

HARNESSING ADVERSITY FOR GROWTH

Adopt a Growth Mindset: View challenges as opportunities for learning and growth. Embrace the belief that abilities and intelligence can be developed through dedication and effort.

Seek Support: Lean on supportive networks of family, friends, or professionals. Sharing experiences and seeking advice can provide fresh perspectives and coping strategies.

Reflect and Learn: After facing adversity, take time to reflect. Ask:

What did I learn from this experience?

How can I use this knowledge in the future?

What strengths did I discover in myself?

Stay Optimistic: Maintain a hopeful outlook. Believe in your ability to overcome challenges and trust that adversity can lead to positive transformations.

Take Proactive Steps: Instead of being paralyzed by adversity, take proactive measures. Develop action plans, set goals, and work towards solutions.

CONCLUSION

Adversity, while daunting, is an essential component of growth. It molds us, refines us, and propels us to new heights. As the renowned German philosopher Friedrich Nietzsche aptly said, "What does not kill me makes me stronger." By embracing adversity as an opportunity for growth, we not only overcome challenges but also transform them into stepping stones towards a richer, more fulfilling life. In the dance of life, adversity and growth are partners, each shaping the rhythm and trajectory of our journey.

TECHNIQUES FOR MENTAL AND EMOTIONAL FORTITUDE: BUILDING INNER STRENGTH

In the ever-evolving landscape of life, mental and emotional fortitude stands as the bedrock of personal well-being and success. It's the inner strength that allows us to face challenges head-on, navigate emotional turbulence, and emerge stronger. But how does one cultivate this resilience of the mind and heart? This article explores techniques to bolster mental and emotional fortitude, equipping you to handle life's ups and downs with grace and poise.

UNDERSTANDING MENTAL AND EMOTIONAL FORTITUDE

Mental and emotional fortitude refers to the resilience, courage, and inner strength that enable individuals to persevere through challenges, manage stress, and recover from setbacks. It's the psychological armor that shields us from life's adversities.

TECHNIQUES TO ENHANCE MENTAL AND EMOTIONAL FORTITUDE

Mindfulness and Meditation: Regular mindfulness practices, such as meditation, help anchor the mind, fostering a sense of calm and clarity. They teach us to observe our thoughts and emotions without judgment, allowing us to respond rather than react.

Positive Affirmations: Replacing negative self-talk with positive affirmations can rewire the brain, fostering a more optimistic and resilient mindset. Phrases like "I am capable" or "I can handle this" serve as empowering reminders.

Emotional Expression: Bottling up emotions can be detrimental. Find healthy outlets for expression, whether it's talking to a trusted friend, journaling, or engaging in creative activities.

Set Boundaries: Recognize your limits and set clear boundaries. This can mean saying "no" when necessary, taking breaks, or distancing yourself from toxic environments or relationships.

Physical Activity: Regular exercise releases endorphins, the body's natural mood elevators. It also helps in managing stress, anxiety, and depression.

Stay Connected: Foster strong, supportive relationships. Social connections offer emotional support, provide different perspectives, and create a sense of belonging.

Continuous Learning: Embrace a growth mindset. View challenges as opportunities to learn and grow. Seek feedback and be open to change.

Practice Gratitude: Regularly reflecting on and expressing gratitude for life's blessings can shift focus from what's lacking or challenging to what's abundant and positive.

Seek Professional Help: If feelings of overwhelm persist, consider seeking therapy or counseling. Professionals can offer tools, strategies, and perspectives tailored to individual needs.

Limit Exposure to Negativity: Be mindful of the content you consume, whether it's news, social media, or entertainment. Surround yourself with positive influences and uplifting content.

<u>CONCLUSION</u>

Mental and emotional fortitude is not a fixed trait but a dynamic quality that can be nurtured and developed. It's akin to a muscle that grows stronger with consistent training. By integrating the techniques mentioned above into daily life, individuals can build a robust inner foundation, ready to face life's challenges with confidence and resilience. Remember, it's not the absence of adversity but the ability to navigate it that truly defines mental and emotional strength. Equip yourself with the tools of fortitude, and you'll find yourself not just surviving, but thriving amidst life's complexities.

The Power of Habit

UNDERSTANDING HABIT FORMATION: THE SCIENCE BEHIND OUR DAILY ROUTINES

Habits, those automatic behaviors we perform without much thought, play a pivotal role in shaping our lives. From the innocuous, like brushing our teeth every morning, to the more impactful, like daily exercise or frequent procrastination, habits dictate our routines, productivity, and overall well-being. But how do these habits form? And how can we harness this knowledge to cultivate positive behaviors? This article delves into the intricacies of habit formation, offering insights into the science behind our daily routines.

THE HABIT LOOP

At the heart of habit formation lies the "habit loop," a concept popularized by Charles Duhigg in his book "The Power of Habit." This loop consists of three key components:

Cue: This is the trigger that initiates the habit loop. It could be an external event, like an alarm ringing, or an internal feeling, like hunger.

Routine: This is the behavior itself, whether it's hitting the snooze button, grabbing a snack, or going for a run.

Reward: After the routine comes the reward—a positive outcome that reinforces the behavior. This could be the relief of getting a few more minutes of sleep, the satisfaction of a tasty treat, or the endorphin rush after a workout.

Over time, as this loop repeats, the brain starts to associate the cue with the reward, making the routine more automatic and less conscious.

THE ROLE OF THE BRAIN

The basal ganglia, a region of the brain associated with emotions, patterns, and memories, plays a crucial role in habit formation. As behaviors become habitual, the brain shifts the control of these actions to the basal ganglia, conserving mental effort and energy. This is why habits, once formed, can be hard to break—they're deeply ingrained neural pathways.

FORMING NEW HABITS

Understanding the habit loop provides valuable insights into forming new habits:

Start Small: Instead of making drastic changes, start with small, manageable behaviors. This reduces resistance and increases the likelihood of consistency.

Consistent Cues: Establish consistent triggers for your new habit. If you want to start jogging every morning, set a regular alarm or lay out your running shoes the night before.

Immediate Rewards: Ensure there's a tangible or emotional reward immediately after the routine. This could be a tasty post-workout smoothie or simply the satisfaction of ticking off a task.

Repetition: Consistency is key. The more you repeat the habit loop, the stronger the neural pathway becomes, making the behavior more automatic.

Track Progress: Maintain a log or journal to track your progress. Visualizing your consistency can be a powerful motivator.

BREAKING BAD HABITS

Breaking habits involves the same principles but in reverse:

Identify the Cue: Recognize the triggers that lead to the undesired behavior.

Alter the Routine: Once you've identified the cue, replace the negative routine with a positive one.

Change the Reward: Find a new, positive reward that satisfies the craving initiated by the cue but doesn't involve the undesired routine.

CONCLUSION

Habit formation, rooted deeply in our neurology, is a powerful mechanism that shapes our behaviors and, by extension, our lives. By understanding the science behind habits, we can become more intentional about the behaviors we cultivate, steering our lives in the direction of growth, well-being, and success. Remember, while habits might be automatic, the power to shape them lies firmly in our hands.

CRAFTING HABITS THAT PROPEL GROWTH: THE BLUEPRINT FOR PERSONAL EVOLUTION

In the vast tapestry of life, habits are the individual threads that weave together our daily experiences, shaping our character, destiny, and overall well-being. While some habits keep us tethered to mediocrity, others have the power to propel us towards exponential growth. But how do we craft habits that truly catalyze personal evolution? This article delves into the art and science of developing habits that foster growth and transformation.

THE POWER OF GROWTH-ORIENTED HABITS

Growth-oriented habits are behaviors that consistently push us out of our comfort zones, challenge our status quo, and drive us towards continuous improvement. They are the catalysts that transform our potential into tangible progress.

STEPS TO CRAFT GROWTH-PROPELLING HABITS

Define Clear Goals: Before crafting habits, have a clear vision of what you want to achieve. Whether it's personal development, professional success, or mastering a skill, clarity is the foundation upon which habits are built.

Start Small and Specific: While the end goal might be grand, start with small, specific habits. Instead of "I will read more," opt for "I will read 10 pages every night before bed."

Consistency is Key: Growth is a result of consistent effort over time. Prioritize consistency over intensity. It's better to practice a skill for 10 minutes daily than for an hour once a week.

Anchor New Habits to Established Ones: Link your new habit to an existing one. If you're trying to cultivate a meditation practice, do it right after your morning coffee, turning the coffee habit into a cue for meditation.

Track and Reflect: Maintain a journal or use habit-tracking apps to monitor your progress. Regular reflection helps in identifying what's working and what needs adjustment.

Celebrate Milestones: Recognize and celebrate small victories along the way. These celebrations reinforce the habit and provide motivation to continue.

Educate Yourself: The more you understand the benefits of a habit, the more likely you are to stick with it. If your goal is to eat healthily, educate yourself about nutrition and its impact on well-being.

Surround Yourself with Role Models: Being around people who embody the habits you want to cultivate can be incredibly motivating. Their journey can offer insights, inspiration, and practical tips.

Embrace Setbacks as Learning Opportunities: No journey is without setbacks. Instead of getting disheartened, view them as feedback. Analyze what went wrong, adjust, and move forward with renewed vigor.

Visualize the End Result: Regularly visualize the positive changes these habits will bring about. This mental imagery serves as fuel, driving you towards your goals.

THE RIPPLE EFFECT OF GROWTH HABITS

One of the most profound aspects of growth-oriented habits is their ripple effect. As you cultivate one positive habit, its benefits often spill over, influencing other areas of your life. For instance, the discipline developed from a regular exercise routine might enhance your work ethic or the patience cultivated from meditation might improve your interpersonal relationships.

CONCLUSION

Crafting habits that propel growth is an investment in oneself. It's a commitment to personal evolution, to becoming the best version of oneself. While the journey might be challenging, the rewards—enhanced skills, improved well-being, and a life of purpose and fulfillment—are well worth the effort. As Aristotle wisely stated, "We are what we repeatedly do. Excellence, then, is not an act, but a habit." Commit to crafting habits that pave the way for growth, and watch as your life transforms in ways you had only imagined.

<u>CHAPTER 6:</u>

Lifelong Learning

The Importance of Continuous Education: Lifelong Learning in a Rapidly Changing World

In an era marked by technological advancements, shifting global dynamics, and an ever-evolving job market, the traditional model of education—where learning ends upon graduation—is quickly becoming obsolete. Continuous education, or the pursuit of knowledge and skills throughout one's life, is no longer just a luxury but a necessity for personal and professional growth. This article delves into the significance of lifelong learning in our contemporary world.

THE CHANGING LANDSCAPE OF LEARNING

The 21st century has ushered in a revolution in how we access, process, and utilize information. With the digital age, knowledge is at our fingertips, industries are in constant flux, and the skills needed yesterday might be redundant tomorrow. In this dynamic environment, continuous education emerges as the key to staying relevant and competitive.

WHY CONTINUOUS EDUCATION MATTERS

Adapting to a Changing Job Market: Automation, artificial intelligence, and technological innovations are reshaping industries. Continuous education ensures that individuals remain employable by staying updated with the latest skills and knowledge.

Personal Growth and Fulfillment: Beyond professional needs, learning new skills or subjects can provide personal satisfaction, stimulate the mind, and enhance one's quality of life.

Problem Solving and Innovation: With a broader knowledge base and diverse skills, individuals are better equipped to approach problems creatively and innovate.

Building Confidence: Mastering new skills or subjects boosts self-confidence, making individuals more assertive in both personal and professional spheres.

Staying Mentally Active: Continuous learning challenges the brain, keeping it sharp. Studies have shown that lifelong learning can even delay cognitive decline in older adults.

Networking: Engaging in courses or workshops can help individuals connect with peers, mentors, or industry leaders, expanding their professional network.

WAYS TO ENGAGE IN CONTINUOUS EDUCATION

Online Courses: Platforms like Coursera, Udemy, and Khan Academy offer courses on a plethora of subjects, allowing individuals to learn at their own pace.

Workshops and Seminars: These provide hands-on experience and direct interaction with experts.

Reading: Books, journals, or reputable online publications can offer deep insights into a subject.

Podcasts and Webinars: These are excellent tools for learning on-the-go, offering flexibility.

Returning to School: Depending on one's goals, pursuing an additional degree or certification might be beneficial.

Engaging in Discussions: Joining clubs or groups that focus on discussions can stimulate thought and offer diverse perspectives.

CONCLUSION

Continuous education is the compass that navigates us through the labyrinth of the modern world. It's the tool that equips us to face challenges head-on, seize opportunities, and craft a path of growth and success. As the renowned futurist Alvin Toffler aptly stated, "The illiterate of the 21st century will not be those who cannot read and write, but those who cannot learn, unlearn, and relearn." Embrace continuous education as a lifelong journey, and you'll find yourself not just surviving but thriving in this ever-changing world.

Tools and Techniques for Effective Learning: Maximizing Knowledge Absorption and Retention

In the vast realm of education and self-improvement, not all learning methods are created equal. While the sheer volume of information available today is staggering, the ability to effectively absorb, process, and retain this information is what truly sets successful learners apart. This article delves into the tools and techniques that can enhance the learning experience, ensuring that time spent studying is both productive and rewarding.

UNDERSTANDING EFFECTIVE LEARNING

Effective learning goes beyond mere memorization. It involves understanding concepts deeply, connecting new information to prior knowledge, and being able to apply what's learned in practical or novel situations.

TOOLS AND TECHNIQUES FOR ENHANCED LEARNING

Active Recall: Instead of passively rereading material, test yourself. Active recall, or the act of retrieving information from memory, strengthens neural pathways and enhances retention.

Spaced Repetition: Instead of cramming, review material at increasing intervals over time. This leverages the psychological spacing effect, improving long-term retention.

Mind Mapping: Use visual diagrams to represent and connect ideas, concepts, and information. This helps in organizing complex subjects and seeing the bigger picture.

Mnemonic Devices: Use rhymes, alliteration, or jokes to make information more memorable. This technique leverages the brain's ability to retain creative or humorous content.

Chunking: Break down complex information into smaller, manageable chunks or groups. This makes it easier to process and remember.

Digital Tools: Platforms like Quizlet for flashcards, Anki for spaced repetition, or Coursera for structured courses can enhance the learning experience.

Study Groups: Engaging in group discussions can offer diverse perspectives, clarify doubts, and reinforce understanding.

Pomodoro Technique: Use a timer to break study sessions into focused intervals (typically 25 minutes), followed by short breaks. This maintains high levels of concentration and reduces cognitive fatigue.

Interleaved Learning: Instead of focusing on one topic for a long duration, mix different topics or subjects. This technique can improve the ability to differentiate between concepts and enhance problem-solving skills.

Real-world Application: Apply what you've learned in practical scenarios. Whether it's practicing a new language with a native speaker or coding a small program, real-world application solidifies understanding.

Stay Curious: Cultivate a mindset of curiosity. Asking questions, exploring related topics, or delving deeper into subjects can enhance comprehension and retention.

Feedback Loop: Regularly assess your understanding through tests, quizzes, or discussions. Feedback highlights areas of strength and those needing further attention.

CONCLUSION

Effective learning is both an art and a science. While the tools and techniques mentioned above provide a roadmap, it's essential to remember that everyone's learning journey is unique. Experiment with different methods, discover what resonates best with you, and continuously refine your approach. In the words of Benjamin Franklin, „An investment in knowledge pays the best interest." Equip yourself with the right tools and techniques, and you'll find that the returns on your learning investments are truly invaluable.

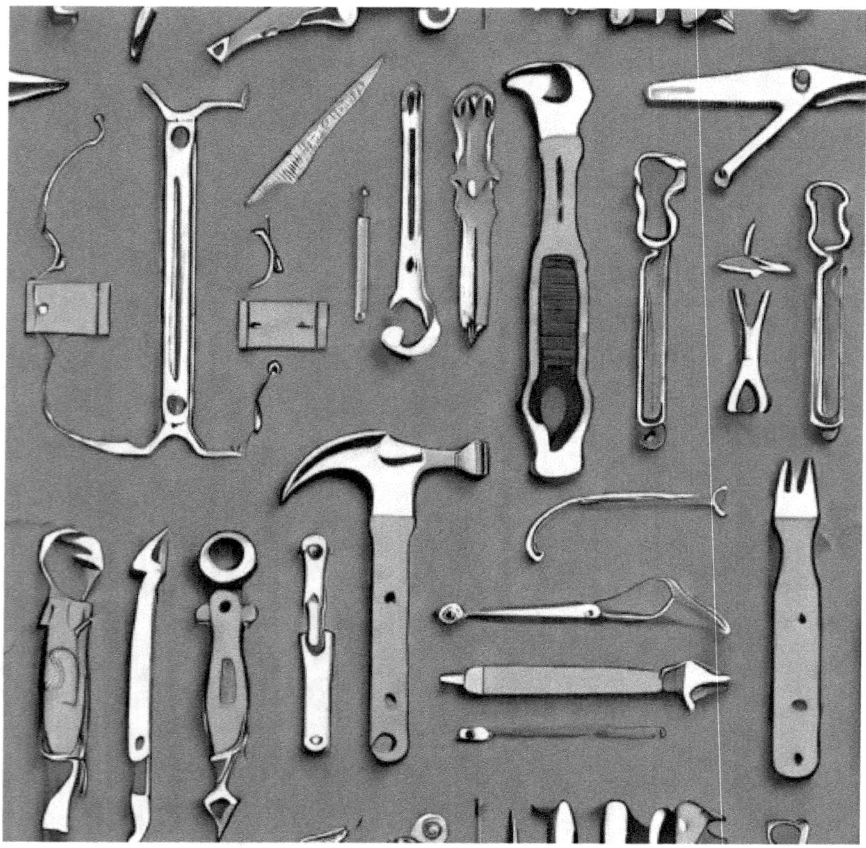

Nurturing Relationships

The Role of Relationships in Personal Growth: Nurturing Bonds that Foster Evolution

Relationships, the intricate web of connections we weave with family, friends, colleagues, and even acquaintances, play a profound role in shaping our lives. While they offer companionship, love, and support, their influence extends far beyond these immediate benefits. Relationships, when nurtured, can be powerful catalysts for personal growth and transformation. This article delves into the multifaceted role relationships play in our journey of self-improvement and evolution.

The Multidimensional Impact of Relationships

Mirror to the Self: Relationships often act as mirrors, reflecting our strengths, weaknesses, beliefs, and behaviors. Through interactions, we gain insights into our patterns, triggers, and areas needing improvement.

Safe Spaces for Vulnerability: Authentic relationships provide safe environments where we can express our fears, dreams, and insecurities. This vulnerability fosters self-awareness and emotional growth.

Challenges and Growth: Disagreements and conflicts, inevitable in any relationship, challenge our perspectives and push us out of our comfort zones. Navigating these challenges cultivates skills like empathy, patience, and effective communication.

Diverse Perspectives: Interacting with individuals from varied backgrounds and experiences broadens our horizons. It exposes us to different viewpoints, encouraging open-mindedness and adaptability.

Support and Encouragement: Relationships offer a support system, providing encouragement during setbacks and celebrating successes. This emotional backing boosts confidence and resilience.

CULTIVATING RELATIONSHIPS THAT PROPEL GROWTH

Open Communication: Foster open and honest communication. Discuss feelings, aspirations, and concerns, ensuring mutual understanding and trust.

Active Listening: Listen to understand, not just to respond. Active listening deepens connections and offers insights into others' perspectives.

Set Boundaries: Recognize and communicate personal boundaries. Healthy boundaries ensure mutual respect and prevent feelings of resentment or burnout.

Invest Time: Quality time strengthens bonds. Engage in shared activities, deep conversations, or even simple moments of togetherness.

Seek Feedback: Encourage loved ones to provide feedback on your behavior, aspirations, or challenges. This external perspective can offer invaluable insights.

Nurture Self-growth: Personal growth enhances relationship quality. By working on oneself, we bring a more evolved, understanding, and compassionate self to our interactions.

THE RIPPLE EFFECT OF GROWTH-ORIENTED RELATIONSHIPS

Relationships that foster growth have a ripple effect, influencing not just the individuals involved but also their extended networks. As individuals evolve, they inspire change in their families, workplaces, and communities. This collective growth paves the way for more harmonious, understanding, and progressive societies.

CONCLUSION

Relationships, in their essence, are more than just bonds between individuals. They are dynamic ecosystems that, when nurtured, have the power to catalyze profound personal growth. As the renowned psychologist Carl Rogers stated, "The curious paradox is that when I accept myself just as I am, then I can change." In relationships, we find both acceptance and the stimulus for change. By recognizing and harnessing the transformative power of relationships, we set ourselves on a path of continuous evolution, enriching not just our lives but also those of everyone we touch.

Building and Maintaining Meaningful Connections: The Art of Authentic Relationships

In a world increasingly dominated by digital interactions and fleeting engagements, the value of meaningful connections has never been more pronounced. These deep, authentic relationships—whether with family, friends, colleagues, or even new acquaintances—enrich our lives, offering support, understanding, and a sense of belonging. But how does one build and maintain such connections in today's fast-paced world? This article delves into the nuances of forging and nurturing relationships that stand the test of time.

THE ESSENCE OF MEANINGFUL CONNECTIONS

Meaningful connections transcend surface-level interactions. They are characterized by mutual respect, understanding, trust, and a genuine interest in each other's well-being. Such relationships are not just about taking but also about giving, sharing, and growing together.

Steps to Build Meaningful Connections

Be Present: In any interaction, be fully present. Listen actively, make eye contact, and engage in the conversation without distractions.

Open Up: Vulnerability fosters deeper connections. Share your feelings, aspirations, fears, and experiences. Authenticity invites authenticity.

Empathize: Put yourself in the other person's shoes. Understand their feelings, perspectives, and challenges. Empathy builds trust and deepens bonds.

Invest Time: Quality time is the bedrock of meaningful relationships. Prioritize face-to-face interactions, engage in shared activities, and create memories together.

Communicate Effectively: Clear, open communication prevents misunderstandings and strengthens relationships. Express your feelings, set boundaries, and address concerns promptly.

Show Appreciation: Recognize and appreciate the value each person brings to your life. Small gestures, words of gratitude, or acts of kindness can reinforce bonds.

MAINTAINING MEANINGFUL CONNECTIONS

Regular Check-ins: Even with busy schedules, take the time to check in on loved ones. A simple message or call can keep the connection alive.

Celebrate Milestones: Celebrate birthdays, achievements, and milestones together. Shared joys amplify happiness.

Navigate Conflicts with Care: Disagreements are natural. Address them with patience, understanding, and a willingness to find common ground.

Grow Together: Engage in activities that foster mutual growth, be it attending workshops, traveling, or reading a book together.

Revisit Memories: Reminiscing about shared experiences can rekindle warmth and reinforce the depth of the connection.

Set and Respect Boundaries: Every strong relationship respects personal boundaries. Understand each other's limits and ensure they are not crossed.

THE RIPPLE EFFECT OF MEANINGFUL CONNECTIONS

Meaningful connections have a profound impact on our well-being. They offer emotional support, reduce feelings of loneliness, and enhance our sense of purpose. Moreover, the positivity from such relationships often ripples out, influencing other aspects of our lives and the lives of those around us.

CONCLUSION

Building and maintaining meaningful connections is an art, one that requires effort, understanding, and commitment. In a world where superficiality often takes precedence, choosing depth can be revolutionary. As the saying goes, "It's not about having a lot of friends; it's about having real ones." By investing in authentic relationships, we not only enrich our own lives but also create a network of love, support, and understanding that stands steadfast amidst the ever-changing tides of life.

CHAPTER 8:

The Role of Mentorship

FINDING THE RIGHT MENTOR: GUIDING LIGHTS ON THE PATH TO SUCCESS

In the journey of personal and professional growth, few relationships are as transformative as that of a mentor and mentee. A mentor, with their experience, wisdom, and insights, can offer invaluable guidance, helping individuals navigate challenges, seize opportunities, and realize their full potential. But how does one find the right mentor? This article delves into the nuances of identifying and building a mentorship relationship that truly catalyzes growth.

THE ESSENCE OF A MENTOR

A mentor is more than just an experienced individual. They are a coach, guide, confidant, and sometimes, a critic. They offer perspective, share knowledge, and provide support, all while challenging the mentee to step out of their comfort zone and aim higher.

STEPS TO FIND THE RIGHT MENTOR

Self-Assessment: Before seeking a mentor, understand your own needs. What are your goals? What challenges are you facing? What skills or knowledge are you seeking? A clear understanding of your objectives will guide your search.

Look Within Your Network: Often, potential mentors are already within your existing network. Think about colleagues, professors, industry contacts, or community leaders you admire.

Industry Events and Workshops: Attend conferences, seminars, and workshops related to your field. Such events often provide opportunities to meet experienced professionals and potential mentors.

Leverage Online Platforms: Websites like LinkedIn or industry-specific forums can be valuable platforms to connect with potential mentors. Engage in discussions, share your insights, and build connections.

Seek Compatibility: A mentor-mentee relationship is deeply personal. Beyond professional alignment, ensure there's a personal compatibility in terms of values, communication styles, and expectations.

Be Proactive: Don't wait for a mentor to find you. Take the initiative to approach potential mentors, express your admiration for their work, and articulate why you believe they'd be a good mentor for you.

Join Mentorship Programs: Many organizations, institutions, and professional bodies offer formal mentorship programs. Enrolling in such programs can streamline the mentor-finding process.

BUILDING A FRUITFUL MENTORSHIP RELATIONSHIP

Set Clear Expectations: At the onset, discuss and define the objectives of the mentorship. Whether it's career guidance, skill development, or networking opportunities, having clear goals ensures a focused mentorship journey.

Respect Their Time: Mentors often juggle multiple commitments. Be punctual for meetings, come prepared, and be concise in your communications.

Seek Feedback and Act on It: A mentor's feedback is invaluable. Actively seek it, be open to it, and, most importantly, act on it.

Maintain Open Communication: Ensure there's a two-way communication channel. Share your progress, challenges, and any changes in your goals or circumstances.

Reciprocate: While the mentor offers guidance and support, remember that mentorship can be a two-way street. Share your insights, offer fresh perspectives, or assist them in areas where you have expertise.

CONCLUSION

Finding the right mentor can be a pivotal milestone in one's growth journey. It's a partnership that, when nurtured, can lead to profound personal and professional evolution. As the ancient Chinese philosopher Confucius stated, "When we see men of worth, we should think of equaling them; when we see men of a contrary character, we should turn inwards and examine ourselves." In the right mentor, we find both inspiration and the challenge to continuously better ourselves. Seek, cherish, and nurture this relationship, and watch as it illuminates the path to success.

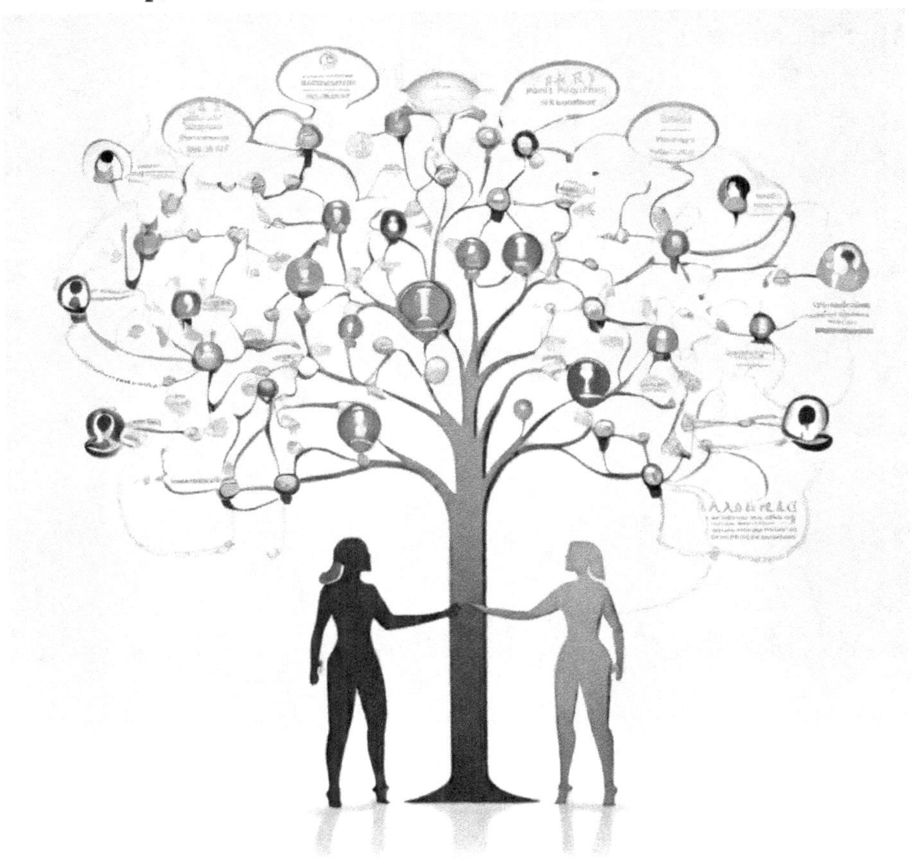

BEING A MENTOR: GIVING BACK AND SHAPING FUTURES

The journey of personal and professional growth is often marked by individuals who guide, inspire, and challenge us. While many of us have benefited from the wisdom of mentors, there comes a time when the torch needs to be passed on. Stepping into the role of a mentor is not just about giving back; it's about shaping the future, one individual at a time. This article explores the profound impact of being a mentor and the ripple effect it creates in the vast ocean of human potential.

THE ESSENCE OF BEING A MENTOR

A mentor is more than just an experienced individual or a guide. They are a beacon, illuminating the path for others, sharing their wisdom, experiences, and insights, and helping mentees navigate the complex maze of life and career.

THE IMPACT OF BEING A MENTOR

Personal Growth: While mentoring is often seen as a one-way street, mentors stand to gain immensely. They develop enhanced leadership skills, gain new perspectives, and often find themselves revisiting and solidifying their own knowledge.

Legacy Building: Through mentoring, one's experiences, values, and insights are passed on, creating a legacy that transcends time. It's a way to make a lasting impact on individuals and industries.

Strengthening Communities: Mentors play a pivotal role in building stronger, more informed communities. They foster growth, innovation, and collaboration, driving collective progress.

Enhanced Satisfaction: There's a profound sense of satisfaction in witnessing the growth and success of mentees. It reaffirms the mentor's journey and the value of their experiences.

Building Networks: Mentoring allows for the expansion of professional and personal networks. Today's mentees could be tomorrow's industry leaders, collaborators, or partners.

TIPS FOR BEING AN EFFECTIVE MENTOR

Listen Actively: While sharing insights is crucial, equally important is the ability to listen. Understand the aspirations, challenges, and perspectives of the mentee.

Be Genuine: Authenticity is the cornerstone of a successful mentor-mentee relationship. Be genuine in your feedback, intentions, and interactions.

Set Boundaries: Define the scope and boundaries of the mentorship. Whether it's the time commitment, areas of guidance, or modes of communication, clarity prevents misunderstandings.

Challenge and Inspire: Go beyond just guidance. Challenge the mentee to step out of their comfort zone, set higher benchmarks, and aspire for more.

Share Failures, Not Just Successes: While successes offer inspiration, failures offer invaluable lessons. Share your challenges, mistakes, and the lessons they brought.

Stay Updated: To offer relevant guidance, mentors need to stay updated with industry trends, advancements, and shifts.

Encourage Independence: The goal of mentoring is not to create a dependent relationship but to empower the mentee to make informed decisions and chart their own course.

CONCLUSION

Being a mentor is a privilege and a responsibility. It's an opportunity to give back, shape futures, and create a legacy that resonates through time. As John C. Crosby aptly stated, "Mentoring is a brain to pick, an ear to listen, and a push in the right direction." Embrace the role of a mentor, and you'll find that while you're shaping the future of your mentee, you're also enriching your own journey in ways you hadn't imagined.

CHAPTER 9:

HEALTH AND WELL-BEEING

THE MIND-BODY CONNECTION: THE INTRICATE DANCE OF THOUGHTS, EMOTIONS, AND PHYSICAL HEALTH

The ancient Greek philosopher Plato once said, "The part can never be well unless the whole is well." This statement encapsulates the essence of the mind-body connection, a concept that has been explored for centuries across cultures, philosophies, and medical traditions. Today, modern science is uncovering the profound ways in which our mental and emotional states influence our physical well-being. This article delves into the intricate relationship between the mind and body, shedding light on how this connection impacts our overall health and well-being.

UNDERSTANDING THE MIND-BODY CONNECTION

The mind-body connection posits that our thoughts, feelings, beliefs, and attitudes can positively or negatively influence our biological functioning. Conversely, what we do with our physical body—what we eat, how much we exercise, even our posture—can impact our mental state.

THE SCIENCE BEHIND THE CONNECTION

Stress and Immunity: Chronic stress, stemming from negative emotions or thoughts, can suppress the immune system, making the body more susceptible to infections and diseases. On the flip side, positive emotions can boost our immune response.

Brain Chemistry: Emotions and thoughts can influence the release of hormones and neurotransmitters. For instance, positive thoughts can trigger the release of endorphins, the body's natural painkillers.

Gut-Brain Axis: Recent research has highlighted the bidirectional communication between the gut and the brain. Our gut health, influenced by diet and lifestyle, can impact our mental state, and vice versa.

Heart Health: Prolonged stress or anxiety can elevate blood pressure and increase the risk of heart disease. On the other hand, practices like meditation and deep breathing can promote heart health.

HARNESSING THE MIND-BODY CONNECTION

Mindfulness and Meditation: Regular mindfulness practices can reduce stress, improve emotional well-being, and even bring about positive physiological changes, such as reduced blood pressure.

Physical Activity: Regular exercise releases endorphins, reducing feelings of anxiety and depression. It also improves cognitive function and overall mental well-being.

Balanced Diet: A nutritious diet not only supports physical health but also mental well-being. Foods rich in omega-3 fatty acids, for instance, can boost brain health and mood.

Positive Affirmations: Cultivating a positive mindset through affirmations can improve mental well-being and, over time, create positive changes in the body.

Holistic Therapies: Practices like yoga, tai chi, and acupuncture have been shown to promote both mental and physical health by balancing the body's energy and enhancing the mind-body connection.

Seeking Support: Therapy, counseling, or support groups can address mental and emotional challenges, leading to improved physical health.

CONCLUSION

The mind-body connection underscores the holistic nature of health. It's a reminder that we aren't just physical entities but a complex blend of thoughts, emotions, and biological processes. By nurturing both our mental and physical well-being, we can achieve a state of balance, where the mind and body work in harmony, leading to optimal health and vitality. As the journey of understanding this connection continues, one thing remains clear: the mind and body are not separate; what affects one, affects the other. Embracing this interconnectedness is the key to a holistic approach to health and well-being.

THE IMPORTANCE OF PRACTICES FOR PHYSICAL, MENTAL, AND SPIRITUAL HEALTH

The intricate tapestry of human existence is woven from threads of physical, mental, and spiritual dimensions. Each dimension, while distinct, deeply influences and is influenced by the others. Cultivating practices that nurture each of these aspects is essential for a multitude of reasons:

HOLISTIC WELL-BEING:

Physical Health: The body is our tangible vessel, enabling us to interact with the world. Maintaining its health ensures we can perform daily activities with vigor, resist illnesses, and enjoy a longer, more active life.

Mental Health: Our mental state governs our thoughts, emotions, and reactions. A healthy mind allows us to process information, make decisions, handle stress, and form healthy relationships.

Spiritual Health: This dimension provides a sense of purpose, connection, and understanding of the larger universe. It offers solace in times of distress, guiding principles for life, and a deeper sense of fulfillment.

INTERCONNECTEDNESS:

Ailments or imbalances in one dimension can manifest symptoms in another. For instance, chronic physical pain can lead to depression, while prolonged stress (a mental factor) can result in physical ailments like heart disease.

<u>ENHANCED QUALITY OF LIFE:</u>

Regular practices that promote health in these areas not only increase longevity but also enhance the quality of life. This means more years of feeling good, being active, and enjoying what life has to offer.

RESILIENCE AND ADAPTABILITY:

Cultivating these three dimensions equips individuals with the tools to face life's challenges. It fosters resilience to bounce back from setbacks and adaptability to navigate changing circumstances.

<u>## PERSONAL GROWTH AND EVOLUTION:</u>

Engaging in practices for physical, mental, and spiritual health facilitates personal growth. It encourages self-awareness, introspection, and a continuous journey towards becoming the best version of oneself.

<u>## POSITIVE SOCIAL IMPACT:</u>

Individuals who are balanced and healthy in these dimensions often radiate positivity, impacting their families, communities, and societies. They tend to be more compassionate, understanding, and collaborative, fostering harmonious relationships and communities.

<u>LEGACY AND CONTRIBUTION:</u>

By prioritizing these practices, individuals often lead by example, inspiring others to also prioritize their well-being. This creates a ripple effect, influencing current and future generations to lead healthier, more fulfilled lives.

CONCLUSION

The importance of practices for physical, mental, and spiritual health cannot be overstated. They are the pillars supporting the edifice of our existence. By nurturing each dimension, we not only enhance our individual lives but also contribute positively to the broader tapestry of human society and the world at large. In essence, these practices are the keys to unlocking a life of harmony, purpose, and profound fulfillment.

<u>30 Practices for Physical, Mental, and Spiritual Health</u>

Holistic well-being encompasses the harmony of body, mind, and spirit. Here are 30 practices that can guide you towards achieving a balanced and enriched life:

PHYSICAL HEALTH:

Consistent Exercise: Incorporate a mix of aerobic, strength, and flexibility exercises into your routine.

Nutrient-Rich Diet: Prioritize whole foods, including vegetables, fruits, lean proteins, and whole grains.

Quality Sleep: Ensure 7-9 hours of uninterrupted sleep to rejuvenate your body.

Stay Hydrated: Drink ample water daily to support metabolism and detoxification.

Routine Health Check-ups: Regularly visit healthcare professionals to monitor and maintain optimal health.

Limit Toxins: Minimize consumption of processed foods, alcohol, and tobacco.

Active Breaks: Incorporate short breaks during work to stretch or take a brief walk.

Posture Awareness: Maintain good posture, especially if working at a desk, to prevent musculoskeletal issues.

Limit Caffeine: Moderate caffeine intake to avoid sleep disturbances and anxiety.

Skin Care: Protect your skin from excessive sun exposure and keep it hydrated.

MENTAL HEALTH:

Mindfulness Meditation: Practice being present to reduce stress and enhance focus.

Digital Detox: Set specific times where you disconnect from electronic devices.

Continuous Learning: Stimulate your brain with activities like reading, puzzles, or new hobbies.

Journaling: Document your thoughts and feelings to process emotions and gain insights.

Positive Affirmations: Reinforce a constructive mindset with uplifting statements.

Seek Counseling: Consider therapy to address emotional or psychological challenges.

Limit News Consumption: Stay informed but avoid excessive exposure to potentially distressing news.

Engage in Art: Explore creative outlets like painting, music, or writing to express and heal.

Practice Gratitude: Regularly acknowledge the positive aspects of your life.

Time Management: Organize your day efficiently to reduce stress and enhance productivity.

SPIRITUAL HEALTH:

Daily Reflection: Dedicate quiet moments for introspection and self-awareness.

Nature Connection: Spend time outdoors to ground yourself and appreciate the natural world.

Gratitude Journaling: Document things you're grateful for to foster a positive outlook.

Prayer or Rituals: Engage in spiritual practices that resonate with your beliefs.

Join Spiritual Communities: Connect with groups or individuals sharing your spiritual journey.

Read Inspirational Literature: Dive into spiritual texts, philosophies, or inspirational writings.

Practice Forgiveness: Let go of grudges and resentments to free your spirit.

Yoga: Combine physical postures with breathwork and meditation for holistic well-being.

Deep Breathing Exercises: Use breath control to calm the mind and connect with your inner self.

Seek Spiritual Guidance: Consider seeking mentors or guides to deepen your spiritual understanding and practices.

By integrating these practices into your daily life, you can nurture each facet of your being, leading to a more balanced, fulfilled, and harmonious existence.

CHAPTER 10:

Celebrating Milestones

THE IMPORTANCE OF RECOGNIZING ACHIEVEMENTS: CELEBRATING MILESTONES ON THE PATH TO SUCCESS

In the relentless pursuit of goals and aspirations, it's easy to become fixated on the destination and overlook the journey. However, pausing to recognize and celebrate achievements, both big and small, is crucial for a multitude of reasons. This article delves into the significance of acknowledging accomplishments and the profound impact it has on individuals and organizations alike.

BOOSTS MOTIVATION AND MORALE:

Recognizing achievements acts as a powerful motivator. It reinforces the belief that hard work and dedication yield results. For individuals, it reignites passion and drive, and in organizational settings, it boosts team morale, fostering a positive and productive work environment.

<u>REINFORCES POSITIVE BEHAVIOR:</u>

When accomplishments are acknowledged, it sets a precedent. It signals the kind of behavior, work ethic, or values that are appreciated and rewarded, encouraging repetition of such positive actions in the future.

<u>ENHANCES SELF-WORTH
AND CONFIDENCE:</u>

Recognition validates effort and skill, enhancing an individual's self-worth. It builds confidence, empowering individuals to take on bigger challenges and push their boundaries.

ENCOURAGES REFLECTION AND GROWTH:

Taking a moment to recognize achievements also offers an opportunity for reflection. It allows individuals and teams to assess what worked, what didn't, and how they can improve or innovate in future endeavors.

STRENGTHENS RELATIONSHIPS AND TEAM DYNAMICS:

In organizational settings, recognizing achievements fosters a culture of appreciation. It strengthens interpersonal relationships and team dynamics, as individuals feel seen, valued, and integral to the collective success.

ATTRACTS TALENT AND RETAINS TOP PERFORMERS:

Organizations that regularly celebrate achievements and milestones are more likely to attract and retain top talent. Recognition is a key factor in job satisfaction and can significantly influence an employee's decision to stay with or leave an organization.

OFFERS CLOSURE AND SETS THE STAGE FOR NEW GOALS:

Recognizing an achievement provides a sense of closure to one chapter, allowing individuals and teams to set their sights on new goals. It's a cyclical process where the end of one journey becomes the starting point for the next.

<u>ENHANCES OVERALL WELL-BEING:</u>

On a psychological level, recognition releases dopamine, a neurotransmitter associated with pleasure and satisfaction. This not only enhances mood but also contributes to overall well-being and mental health.

CONCLUSION

Recognizing achievements is not just about celebrating success; it's about valuing effort, resilience, and determination. It's a testament to the journey, with all its challenges, learnings, and growth. In a world that often emphasizes shortcomings and areas of improvement, taking the time to acknowledge and celebrate accomplishments becomes a beacon of positivity. It reminds us that every step, no matter how small, is a stride towards progress, deserving of recognition and applause.

SETTING NEW GOALS AFTER ACHIEVEMENTS: THE CONTINUOUS JOURNEY OF GROWTH AND EVOLUTION

Achieving a goal is a moment of triumph, a testament to one's dedication, hard work, and perseverance. But what happens after the euphoria of accomplishment fades? For many, the post-achievement phase can be a mix of contentment, reflection, and even a touch of aimlessness. It's essential to harness this transitional period to set new goals, ensuring that personal or professional growth doesn't stagnate. This article delves into the importance of setting new goals after achievements and offers insights into navigating this crucial phase.

THE NATURE OF GROWTH:

Growth is not a destination but a continuous journey. Just as a tree doesn't stop growing after bearing its first fruit, individuals shouldn't halt their progress after achieving a particular goal. New goals provide direction, purpose, and a renewed sense of challenge.

<u>AVOIDING COMPLACENCY:</u>

Resting on one's laurels can lead to complacency. While it's essential to celebrate and relish achievements, it's equally crucial to recognize that the world is dynamic. To remain relevant, competitive, or fulfilled, one must continuously evolve, adapt, and aim higher.

<u>## BUILDING ON PREVIOUS SUCCESSES:</u>

Every achievement provides a foundation to build upon. The skills acquired, the lessons learned, and the confidence gained can be leveraged to tackle more significant challenges and pursue loftier goals.

<u>SETTING SMART GOALS:</u>

When setting new goals, ensure they are Specific, Measurable, Achievable, Relevant, and Time-bound (SMART). This framework provides clarity, direction, and a tangible roadmap for achieving the next milestone.

<u>SEEKING INSPIRATION:</u>

Look around for inspiration. It could come from peers, mentors, books, or even personal reflections. Sometimes, understanding what others are achieving or recognizing gaps in one's own journey can provide the impetus for the next goal.

EMBRACING A GROWTH MINDSET:

Cultivate a growth mindset, where challenges are viewed as opportunities rather than obstacles. This mindset fosters resilience, adaptability, and a continuous thirst for learning and growth.

<u>PERIODIC REVIEWS:</u>

Once new goals are set, it's essential to periodically review and assess progress. Regular check-ins ensure that one remains on track and can make necessary adjustments based on changing circumstances or new insights.

<u>CELEBRATING SMALL WINS:</u>
While the focus might be on a larger goal, it's crucial to acknowledge and celebrate smaller milestones along the way. These mini-celebrations boost morale, motivation, and provide a sense of progress.

<u>SEEKING FEEDBACK:</u>

Engage with mentors, peers, or team members to get feedback on your new goals. External perspectives can offer valuable insights, validate your direction, or highlight areas of improvement.

CONCLUSION

Setting new goals after achievements is the heartbeat of continuous growth. It's a cycle where the end of one journey seamlessly merges with the beginning of another. As the renowned motivational speaker Les Brown aptly said, "Life takes on meaning when you become motivated, set goals and charge after them in an unstoppable manner." So, after every achievement, take a moment to bask in the glory, reflect, and then set your sights on the next horizon. The journey of growth and evolution is endless, and each goal is but a stepping stone in this grand adventure.

....and it continues..keep pushing!

THE JOURNEY CONTINUES: EMBRACING A LIFE OF GROWTH

Life is often likened to a journey, a metaphorical path filled with twists, turns, peaks, and valleys. But what truly defines this journey is not the destination we're aiming for, but the continuous growth and evolution we undergo along the way. "The Journey Continues" is not just a phrase; it's a philosophy, a way of life that emphasizes the importance of embracing growth at every stage of our existence. This article delves into the essence of this journey and the beauty of a life committed to perpetual growth.

GROWTH: A LIFELONG ENDEAVOR

From the moment we take our first breath to our last, growth is an intrinsic part of our existence. As infants, we grow physically and mentally, learning to interact with the world around us. As adults, our growth might be less tangible but is equally significant. It manifests in the form of personal development, learning new skills, overcoming challenges, and expanding our horizons.

THE BEAUTY OF UNFINISHED STORIES

A life of continuous growth means that our story is always unfolding, always in progress. There's beauty in the 'unfinished' – it signifies potential, hope, and endless possibilities. It's a reminder that no matter our age or stage in life, there's always more to learn, explore, and achieve.

EMBRACING CHANGE

One of the fundamental aspects of growth is change. To grow is to change, evolve, and transform. While change can be daunting, it's also invigorating. It pushes us out of our comfort zones, challenges our perceptions, and paves the way for new experiences and insights.

THE ROLE OF CHALLENGES

Growth is seldom a product of comfort and complacency. It's the challenges, setbacks, and failures that truly shape us. They teach resilience, perseverance, and humility. By embracing these challenges and learning from them, we fuel our journey of growth.

CONTINUOUS LEARNING

A commitment to growth inherently means a commitment to continuous learning. It's about staying curious, asking questions, and seeking knowledge. Whether it's picking up a new hobby, diving into a book, or traveling to a new destination, every experience adds a new chapter to our growth story.

THE RIPPLE EFFECT OF GROWTH

Personal growth doesn't just benefit the individual; it has a ripple effect. As we grow, we influence and inspire those around us. We contribute more effectively to our communities, workplaces, and families. Our growth journey, in turn, becomes a beacon for others to embark on their own.

CONCLUSION

"The Journey Continues: Embracing a Life of Growth" is a call to action for each one of us. It's an invitation to view life not as a finite game with a set endpoint but as an infinite game filled with endless opportunities for growth and exploration. As we traverse this journey, let's cherish each step, celebrate the milestones, and always remain open to the boundless potential that lies ahead. For in the pursuit of growth, we discover not just our best selves, but the true essence and adventure of life.

APPENDICES

<u>5 SELF-GROWTH EXERCISES AND WORKSHEETS</u>

1. Self-Reflection Journaling Exercise

Objective: To encourage introspection and identify areas of personal growth.

Worksheet:

Date:

Today's Achievements:

Challenges Faced:

Emotions Felt Today:

Lessons Learned:

Goals for Tomorrow:

2. SWOT Analysis for Personal Growth

Objective: To identify Strengths, Weaknesses, Opportunities, and Threats in one's personal life.

Worksheet:

Strengths: (List personal strengths, e.g., communication skills, resilience)

1.

2.

3.

Weaknesses: (List areas of improvement or vulnerabilities)

1.

2.

3.

Opportunities: (List potential chances for growth, e.g., a new course, networking events)

1.

2.

3.

Threats: (List external factors that could hinder personal growth, e.g., toxic relationships, work environment)

1.

2.

3.

3. Gratitude Exercise

Objective: To cultivate a positive mindset and appreciate life's blessings.

Worksheet:

Date:

Three Things I'm Grateful for Today:

1.

2.

3.

One Person I'm Thankful for Today and Why:

4. Goal Setting and Action Plan

Objective: To set clear, achievable goals and create a roadmap to achieve them.

Worksheet:

Long-Term Goal:

Why This Goal is Important:

Short-Term Milestones:

1.

2.

3.

Action Steps for the Next Week:

1.

2.

3.

Potential Challenges and Solutions:

1.

2.

3.

5. Core Values Identification Exercise

Objective: To identify and understand personal core values that guide decisions and behavior.

Worksheet:

List of Potential Values (e.g., honesty, family, freedom, health, creativity, etc.)

Circle 10 values that resonate the most.

Narrow down to your top 5 core values:
1.
2.
3.
4.
5.

For each core value, write a brief description of why

it's important to you.

These exercises and worksheets are designed to encourage introspection, goal-setting, and a deeper understanding of oneself. Regularly engaging in these exercises can provide clarity, direction, and a sense of purpose in one's personal growth journey.

20 RESOURCES AND TOOLS FOR FURTHER EXPLORATION OF SELF-GROWTH

Books:

"The 7 Habits of Highly Effective People" by Stephen R. Covey: A classic guide on productivity and personal effectiveness.

"Mindset: The New Psychology of Success" by Carol S. Dweck: Explores the concept of "fixed" vs. "growth" mindsets and their impact on success.

"Atomic Habits" by James Clear: Offers insights into habit formation and how small changes can lead to significant improvements in one's life.

"The Power of Now" by Eckhart Tolle: Delves into the spiritual aspect of self-growth and the importance of living in the present moment.

ONLINE COURSES:

Coursera: Offers a variety of courses on personal development, from leadership skills to mindfulness practices.

Udemy: Features courses on a range of self-growth topics, including time management, communication skills, and personal branding.

<u>APPS:</u>

Headspace: A meditation app that provides guided sessions to enhance mindfulness and reduce stress.

HabitBull: Helps users track and build positive habits, fostering consistent personal growth.

Reflectly: A journaling app that encourages daily reflection and self-awareness.

MyStrengths: Based on the StrengthsFinder assessment, this app helps users discover and leverage their personal strengths.

<u>PODCASTS:</u>

"The Tim Ferriss Show": Features interviews with top performers from various fields, offering insights into their habits and growth strategies.

"The School of Greatness" with Lewis Howes: Explores the journeys of successful individuals and the lessons they've learned.

<u>WEBSITES AND BLOGS:</u>

MindBodyGreen: Covers a range of topics related to wellness, personal growth, and holistic health.

Tiny Buddha: Offers articles and personal stories on mindfulness, self-growth, and spirituality.

Personal Growth Lab: Focuses on productivity, personal development, and self-improvement strategies.

WORKSHOPS AND SEMINARS:

Landmark Forum: A personal development program that focuses on self-awareness, communication, and leadership.

Tony Robbins' Unleash The Power Within: A multi-day seminar that delves into personal growth, health, and peak performance.

COMMUNITIES AND GROUPS:

Meetup: Allows users to find and join local groups focused on personal growth, from book clubs to meditation circles.

Reddit's r/selfimprovement: A community where individuals share resources, stories, and advice on personal development.

Mastermind Groups: Peer-to-peer mentoring groups where individuals can discuss challenges, set goals, and seek feedback.

Exploring these resources and tools can provide valuable insights, strategies, and support on the journey of self-growth. Whether you're reading a book, taking an online course, or joining a community, each resource offers a unique perspective and approach to personal development.

ACKNOWLEDGMENTS

First and foremost, I extend my deepest gratitude to the universe for its mysterious ways, guiding me on this transformative journey of self-growth and allowing me to share my insights with the world.

To my family, who have been my anchor throughout this journey, your unwavering support and belief in me have been the bedrock upon which I built my dreams. Your lessons, both spoken and unspoken, have shaped my understanding of growth and resilience.

A heartfelt thank you to my mentors and teachers, who, over the years, have illuminated my path with their wisdom, challenging me to question, reflect, and evolve. Your guidance has been invaluable, and your faith in me, a constant source of strength.

I am immensely grateful to my friends and peers, who have been both mirrors and windows in my life. Through our shared experiences, debates, and reflections, you've enriched my perspectives and added depth to my narrative.

Special thanks to my editor, [Editor's Name], whose keen eye and intuitive understanding of the subject helped refine this work into its final form. Your patience, dedication, and insights have been instrumental in bringing this book to life.

I'd also like to acknowledge the countless authors, thinkers, and visionaries in the realm of self-growth whose works have inspired and informed my own. Your pioneering contributions to the field have paved the way for explorers like me.

Lastly, to you, dear reader, thank you for embarking on this journey with me. It is my sincere hope that the pages of this book resonate with you, inspire you, and serve as a beacon on your own path of self-discovery and growth.

<u>WITH GRATITUDE AND LOVE, CHRISI TIAN</u>